Statutory

CODE OF PRACTICE ON THE DUTY TO PROMOTE RACE EQUALITY

COMMISSION FOR
RACIAL EQUALITY

Contents

Foreword

The duty to promote race equality is both an opportunity and a challenge for Britain's public sector. The duty has arisen at a time when our public services are experiencing large-scale modernisation. The drive to improve performance, openness and accountability is rapidly changing the way public authorities work. The new duty now adds the need for fairness.

Since the Stephen Lawrence Inquiry Report identified 'institutional racism' in one of Britain's main public services, many authorities have already reviewed their policies and procedures and have begun the long-term task of overhauling the way they work and think. The new duty will help public authorities remove discrimination – and the possibility of discrimination – from public services, and positively promote race equality in everything they do.

This statutory code of practice aims to help public authorities meet their duty. We have designed it to give them practical guidance on the steps they should take to tackle racial discrimination and promote equal opportunities and good race relations.

You should read this code together with the non-statutory good practice guides we have also produced. These include a general guide for public authorities, one for schools, one for further and higher education institutions, and a general guide to ethnic monitoring. You will find the statutory code of practice, the non-statutory guides, and other useful information on our website (www.cre.gov.uk).

We publish this code and the guides to good practice following wide consultation. We are grateful for the time so many of you took to comment on the drafts, and have tried as far as possible to take account of your concerns and suggestions. We hope that the code and the guides serve you – and race equality – well.

Gurbux Singh

Chair, Commission for Racial Equality

Glossary

action plan

a practical and realistic plan, with an agreed timetable, showing how an authority is planning to meet its duties.

assessing impact

a systematic way of finding out whether a policy (or proposed policy) affects different racial groups differently. This may include obtaining and analysing data, and consulting people, including staff, on the policy.

complementary

this refers to the fact that the three parts of the general duty support each other and may, in practice, overlap. However, they are different, and public authorities should consider each one individually.

consultation

asking for views on policies or services from staff, colleagues, service-users, or the general public. Different circumstances call for different types of consultation. For example, consultation includes meetings, focus groups, reference groups, citizens' juries, surveys, and questionnaires.

direct discrimination

treating one person less favourably than another on racial grounds (see page 5). Direct discrimination is unlawful under the Race Relations Act.

disciplinary procedures

the arrangements and procedures used to discipline staff. These may include informal and formal disciplinary measures.

duty to promote race equality

the general duty (see page 3), unless the context suggests otherwise.

ethnic monitoring

the process you use to collect, store and analyse data about people's ethnic backgrounds.

focus groups, reference groups and citizens' juries

various forms of face-to-face consultation with members of the public, service-users, or others.

formal investigation

an investigation by the CRE under sections 49–52 of the Race Relations Act. The investigation can be either a 'named person' investigation or a general investigation.

- A 'named person' investigation can be carried out if the CRE suspects that an organisation is discriminating on racial grounds. The CRE can ask the organisation for documents and information. If the CRE is satisfied that unlawful discrimination has taken place, or is taking place, the CRE can issue a 'non-discrimination notice'.

- A general investigation can be carried out, without suspicion of discrimination, to examine practice within an area of activity. At the end of the investigation, the CRE can make recommendations.

functions

the full range of a public authority's duties and powers.

further and higher education institution

the governing body of an institution in the further and higher education sectors (as defined in sections 91(3) and 91(5) of the Further and Higher Education Act 1992).

general duty

the duty as given in section 71(1) of the Race Relations Act (see chapter 3, paragraph 3.1).

grievance procedures

arrangements or procedures for dealing with grievances, such as complaints about bullying, harassment or discrimination; or appeals against decisions on promotion or appraisal marks.

indirect racial discrimination

occurs when a rule or condition which is applied equally to everyone:

- can be met by a considerably smaller proportion of people from a particular racial group;

- is to the disadvantage of that group; and

- cannot be justified on non-racial grounds.

All three conditions must apply.

judicial review

a claim to the High Court or the Scottish Court of Sessions asking the court to review the way a public authority or certain other bodies made a decision. The court will not decide the merits of the decision, only whether it is legal. The court can ask the authority to reconsider the matter.

monitoring

the process of collecting, analysing and evaluating information, to measure performance, progress or change.

non-devolved authorities

public authorities in Scotland whose functions and powers remain the responsibility of the Westminster Parliament rather than the Scottish Parliament.

obligatory

this refers to the fact that public authorities are legally bound to meet the general duty, and must make race equality a central part of their functions.

orders

ministerial directions to apply the law, or to change the way it applies.

performance assessment procedures

formal and informal staff appraisals that are likely to affect career development, pay and benefits.

policies

the formal and informal decisions about how a public authority carries out its duties and uses its powers.

positive action

action permitted by the Race Relations Act that allows a person to:

- provide facilities to meet the special needs of people from particular racial groups in relation to their training, education or welfare (section 35); and

- target job training at people from racial groups that are under-represented in a particular area of work, or encourage them to apply for such work (sections 37 and 38).

promoting race equality

public authorities should have 'due regard to the need', in carrying out their functions, to:

- tackle unlawful racial discrimination;

- promote equality of opportunity; and

- promote good relations between people from different racial groups.

proportionate

this refers to the fact that the weight given to race equality should be proportionate to its relevance to a particular function. This approach may mean giving greater consideration and resources to functions or policies that have most effect on the public, or on the authority's employees.

public appointments

appointments to the boards of public bodies. These are bodies that have a role in the processes of national government, but operate at arm's length from government.

public authority

a body named, defined or described in schedule 1A to the Race Relations Act or, depending on the context, a body named, defined or described in one of the schedules to the Race Relations Act 1976 (Statutory Duties) Order 2001.

public functions

functions that affect, or are likely to affect, the public or a section of the public. While only the courts can decide this, public functions would normally not include internal management or contractual matters such as employing staff; purchasing goods, works or services; or buying or selling premises. This term is used to refer to those authorities that are bound by the duties only in relation to their public functions (for example professional representative organisations, such as the Royal College of Surgeons, or broadcasting authorities).

public procurement

the contractual or other arrangements that a public authority makes to obtain goods, works or services from an outside organisation.

publish

making publicly available; for example by producing a written document for distribution.

race equality policy

a written statement of an educational establishment's policy on race equality, which is put into practice and monitored.

race equality scheme

a timetabled and realistic plan, setting out an authority's arrangements for meeting the general and specific duties.

Race Relations Act

the Race Relations Act 1976, as amended by the Race Relations (Amendment) Act 2000.

racial group

a group of people defined by their race, colour, nationality (including citizenship), ethnic or national origins.

racial grounds

reasons of race, colour, nationality (including citizenship), ethnic or national origins.

relevance

this refers to the fact that race equality will be more relevant to some public functions than others. Relevance is about how far a function or policy affects people, as members of the public, and as employees of the authority.

schedule

an appendix to legislation, such as schedule 1A to the Race Relations Act. This schedule lists the public authorities to which the general duty applies.

school

the governing body of an educational establishment maintained by local education authorities in England and Wales, or of a city technology college, a city college for technology of the arts, or a city academy.

Scottish public authority

a public authority whose functions can only be carried out in, or in relation to, Scotland.

specific duty

a duty imposed by the Race Relations Act 1976 (Statutory Duties) Order 2001.

statutory code of practice

a document such as this one, which offers practical guidance on the law, has been approved by Parliament, and is admissible in evidence in a court of law.

statutory duties

duties, either general or specific, which an authority is legally bound to meet.

training

a wide range of career development opportunities, which could include informal in-house training as well as more formal courses.

victimisation

punishing or treating someone unfairly because they have made a complaint of racial discrimination, or are thought to have done so; or because they have supported someone else who has made a complaint of racial discrimination. Victimisation is defined as unlawful discrimination under the Race Relations Act.

Part I

Promoting race
equality in
all listed public
authorities

1

Promoting race equality
Introduction

1.1 The Race Relations Act (see the glossary) places a general duty on a wide range of public authorities to promote race equality. This duty means that authorities (listed in appendix 1 of this code) must have due regard to the need to:

a. eliminate unlawful racial discrimination;

b. promote equality of opportunity; and

c. promote good relations between people of different racial groups.

1.2 Most public authorities are bound by this duty. Many of them provide major public services, such as education or health. Some of them (for example professional representative organisations, such as the Royal College of Surgeons, or broadcasting authorities) are bound by this duty only so far as their public functions (see the glossary) are concerned.

1.3 The duty aims to make the promotion of race equality central to the way public authorities work. Promoting race equality will improve the way public services are delivered for everyone. In most cases, these authorities should be able to use their existing arrangements – such as those for policy making – to meet the duty's requirements. This should help to avoid any unnecessary or duplicated work.

Benefits of the duty

1.4 The duty will help public authorities to make steady progress in achieving race equality. In relation to policy development and service delivery, the duty will:

a. encourage policy makers to be more aware of possible problems;

b. contribute to more informed decision making;

c. make sure that policies are properly targeted;

d. improve the authority's ability to deliver suitable and accessible services that meet varied needs;

e. encourage greater openness about policy making;

f. increase confidence in public services, especially among ethnic minority communities;

g. help to develop good practice; and

h. help to avoid claims of unlawful racial discrimination.

1.5 The duty of public authorities to promote race equality in *employment* will:

a. help to make the authority's workforce more representative of the communities it serves;

b. attract able staff;

c. avoid losing or undervaluing able staff;

d. improve staff morale and productivity;

e. improve the way staff are managed;

f. help to develop good practice; and

g. help to avoid claims of unlawful racial discrimination.

Purpose of the code

1.6 Public authorities can decide how they will meet their duty to promote race equality. The Race Relations Act gives the CRE the power to issue codes of practice, with the approval of Parliament.

1.7 This code offers practical guidance to public authorities on how to meet their duty to promote race equality. It includes guidance on both the general duty (see 1.1) and specific duties imposed by the Home Secretary. The code's aim is to help public authorities to adopt good practice and to eliminate racial discrimination. The code should also help the public understand what public authorities have to do, and the role that the public can play.

1.8 The specific duties imposed by order of the Home Secretary came into effect on **3 December 2001**. Public authorities bound by these duties (see appendices 2, 3 and 4) were required to have properly timetabled and realistic plans for meeting these duties in place by **31 May 2002**.

1.9 This code applies to public authorities in England and Wales (see appendix 1) and to 'non-devolved' public authorities in Scotland (see the glossary and appendix 1). Chapter 6 of this code applies only to the governing bodies of educational institutions in England and Wales. The Code of Practice for Scotland will apply to devolved public authorities in Scotland (see the glossary).

Nature of the code

1.10   This code of practice is a 'statutory' code. This means that it has been approved by Parliament. It also means that the code is admissible in evidence in any legal action, and a court or tribunal should take the code's recommendations into account. On its own, the code does not place any legal obligations on public authorities. It is not a complete statement of the law, as only the courts can give this. If a public authority does not follow the code's guidance, it may need to be able to show how it has otherwise met its legal obligations under the general duty and any specific duties.

How to use this code

1.11   The code is divided into five parts, seven chapters and six appendices.

a.   Part I (chapters 2 and 3) applies to all listed public authorities, including schools, and further and higher education institutions.

b.   Part II (chapters 4 and 5) deals with promoting race equality in certain public authorities other than educational institutions.

c.   Part III (chapter 6) deals with promoting race equality in educational institutions.

d.   Part IV (chapter 7) deals with the CRE's role, including enforcing this code.

e.   Part V (appendices 1 to 6) lists the public authorities that are bound by the general duty (appendix 1), the public authorities that are required to publish a race equality scheme (appendix 2), the public authorities bound by the employment duty (appendix 3), the public authorities bound by the duties for educational institutions (appendix 4), Scottish public authorities (appendix 5), and other guidance published by the CRE (appendix 6).

2

Promoting race equality
The legal framework

2.1 The Race Relations Act (see the glossary) defines direct and indirect discrimination, and victimisation (see the glossary for each of these terms). It outlaws racial discrimination in employment, training, education, housing, public appointments, and the provision of goods, facilities and services. The Race Relations (Amendment) Act 2000 came into force on 2 April 2001 and since then the Race Relations Act (the Act) has covered all the functions of public authorities (with just a few exceptions).

2.2 Section 71(1) of the Act places a general duty on listed public authorities (see appendix 1). The Act also gives the Home Secretary power to make orders placing specific duties on all or some of these authorities (section 71(2)). Scottish ministers have a similar power over Scottish public authorities (section 71B(1); see the glossary). Under the Race Relations Act 1976 (Statutory Duties) Order 2001, the specific duties discussed in this code came into force on **3 December 2001.**

2.3 The Act gives the CRE enforcement powers over the specific duties imposed by the Home Secretary and Scottish ministers. The Act also gives the CRE power to issue codes of practice containing practical guidance on how public authorities can meet the general duty (see chapter 3) and specific duties (see chapters 4, 5 and 6). This is a statutory code, issued for this purpose.

The general duty to promote race equality

2.4 This general duty applies to all public authorities listed in schedule 1A to the Act (see appendix 1). The duty's aim is to make the promotion of race equality central to the work of the listed public authorities.

Specific duties to promote race equality

2.5 Specific duties have been placed on some public authorities responsible for delivering important public services. The duties involve making arrangements that will help these authorities to meet the general duty to promote race equality.

a. The public authorities listed in appendix 2 must prepare and publish a race equality scheme. This scheme should set out the 'functions' or 'policies' (see the glossary for both terms) that are relevant to meeting the general duty, and the arrangements that will help to meet the duty in the areas of policy and service delivery (see chapter 4).

b. The public authorities listed in appendix 3 must monitor their employment procedures and practice (see chapter 5). Some of these authorities have to produce a race equality scheme. They may find it useful to include the arrangements they make to meet their employment duties in their race equality schemes.

c. The educational institutions listed in appendix 4 have to prepare a race equality policy and put in place arrangements for meeting their specific duties on policy and employment (see chapter 6).

2.6 Public authorities that introduce effective arrangements, as required under the specific duties, should be able to show that they are meeting the general duty to promote race equality. Taking action to promote race equality should give authorities the evidence they need to show that they are meeting the general duty.

2.7 Chapters 4, 5, and 6 give guidance on the specific duties.

Liability under the Race Relations Act

2.8 Public authorities are responsible for meeting their general and specific duties. Within each public authority, this responsibility will rest with the groups or individuals who are liable (legally responsible) for the authority's acts or failure to act.

Private or voluntary organisations carrying out a public authority's functions

2.9 When a public authority has a contract or other agreement with a private company or voluntary organisation to carry out any of its functions (see the glossary), and the duty to promote race equality applies to those functions, the public authority remains responsible for meeting the general duty and any specific duties that apply to those functions. The authority should therefore consider the arrangements it will need. If the authority's race equality duties are relevant to the functions it is contracting out, it may be appropriate to incorporate those duties among the performance requirements for delivery of the service. For example, a contractor could be required to monitor service users by their racial group, to make sure the authority is meeting its duties. This would not involve requirements concerning the contractor's internal practices. Whatever action the authority takes, it must be consistent with the policy and legal framework for public procurement.

2.10 In addition to specifications for the general duty and any specific duties, public authorities may promote race equality by encouraging contractors to draw up policies that will help them (contractors) to avoid unlawful discrimination, and promote equality of opportunity. Such encouragement should only be within a voluntary framework, once contracts have been awarded, rather than by making specific criteria or conditions part of the selection process. Public authorities should bear in mind that the general duty does not override other laws or regulations on public procurement. In particular, as above, whatever action the authority takes must be consistent with the policy and legal framework for public procurement.

Partnership

2.11 Public authorities should take account of their general duty to promote race equality – and any specific duties – when they work with other public, private or voluntary organisations. There is no similar obligation on private or voluntary-sector partners.

2.12 Public authorities that are involved in partnership work with other public authorities, or with private or voluntary-sector organisations, are still responsible for meeting their general duty to promote race equality, and any specific duties.

2.13 In practice, this will mean that a public authority working within a partnership will need to seek agreement from its partners to arrangements for planning, funding and managing joint work that will allow it to meet its statutory race equality duties. Public authorities should reflect their partnership work in their race equality schemes.

Inspecting and auditing public authorities

2.14 Agencies that audit or inspect public authorities are bound by the duty to promote race equality. These agencies need to consider how the duty fits with their inspection or audit obligations. In most cases, inspection and audit bodies should be able to use their existing inspection arrangements to promote race equality.

3

Promoting race equality
The general duty

3.1 This chapter explains what public authorities can do to meet the general duty to promote race equality. The duty is set out in section 71(1) of the Race Relations Act (the Act) and it applies to every public authority listed in schedule 1A to the Act (see appendix 1 of this code). Section 71(1) says:

> Every body or other person specified in Schedule 1A or of a description falling within that Schedule shall, in carrying out its functions, have due regard to the need
>
> a) to eliminate unlawful racial discrimination; and
>
> b) to promote equality of opportunity and good relations between persons of different racial groups.*

Guiding principles

3.2 Four principles should govern public authorities' efforts to meet their duty to promote race equality.

a. Promoting race equality is obligatory for all public authorities listed in schedule 1A to the Act (see appendix 1).

b. Public authorities must meet the duty to promote race equality in all relevant functions.

c. The weight given to race equality should be proportionate to its relevance.

d. The elements of the duty are complementary (which means they are all necessary to meet the whole duty).

'Obligatory'

3.3 Public authorities listed in schedule 1A to the Act must make race equality a central part of their functions (such as planning, policy making, service delivery, regulation, inspection, enforcement, and employment). The general duty does not tell public authorities how to do their work, but it expects them to assess whether race equality is relevant to their functions. If it is, the authority should do everything it can to meet the general duty. The duty should underpin all policy and practice, and it should encourage improvement. It is not necessarily a new responsibility for the authority, just a more effective way of doing what it already does.

---

* For immigration and nationality functions, the general duty does not include the words 'equality of opportunity and' (section 71A(1)).

'Relevant'

3.4   Race equality will be more relevant to some functions than others. Relevance is about how much a function affects people, as members of the public or as employees of the authority. For example, a local authority may decide that race equality is more relevant to raising educational standards than to its work on highway maintenance. Public authorities should therefore assess whether, and how, race equality is relevant to each of their functions. A public authority may decide that the general duty does not apply to some of its functions; for example those that are purely technical, such as traffic control or weather forecasting.

'Proportionate'

3.5   Under section 71(1) of the Act, public authorities are expected to have 'due regard' to the three parts of the duty to promote race equality (see 1.1). This means that the weight given to race equality should be proportionate to its relevance to a particular function. In practice, this approach may mean giving greater consideration and resources to functions or policies that have most effect on the public, or on the authority's employees. The authority's concern should be to ask whether particular policies could affect different racial groups in different ways, and whether the policies will promote good race relations.

3.6   'Due regard' does not mean that race equality is less important when the ethnic minority population is small. It is also not acceptable for a public authority to claim that it does not have enough resources to meet the duty. This is because meeting the general duty is a statutory requirement. In practice, this means that public authorities should draw on work they already do to promote race equality, and build on it, using their existing administrative systems and processes and adjusting their plans and priorities, where necessary.

3.7   The general duty is a continuing duty. What a public authority has to do to meet it may change over time as its functions or policies change, or as the communities it serves change.

'Complementary'

3.8   The general duty has three parts:

   a.   eliminating unlawful racial discrimination;

   b.   promoting equality of opportunity; and

   c.   promoting good relations between people of different racial groups.

3.9   These three parts support each other. And, in practice, they may overlap (for example, promoting equality of opportunity may also eliminate or prevent unlawful racial discrimination, *and* promote good race relations). However, it is important to remember that the three parts are different, and that achieving one of them may not lead to achieving all three. For example, a new equal opportunities policy that is not clearly explained when it is introduced may improve equality of opportunity, but it may also damage race relations and create resentment if staff do not understand how it benefits everyone.

3.10   Public authorities should consider and deal with all three parts of the general duty.

How to meet the general duty

3.11   Public authorities should consider the following four steps to meet the general duty.

   a.   Identify which of their functions and policies are relevant to the duty, or, in other words, affect most people.

   b.   Put the functions and policies in order of priority, based on how relevant they are to race equality.

   c.   Assess whether the way these 'relevant' functions and policies are being carried out meets the three parts of the duty.

   d.   Consider whether any changes need to be made to meet the duty, and make the changes.

Identifying relevant functions

3.12   To identify relevant functions, a public authority will find it useful, first, to make a list of all its functions, including employment. It should then assess how relevant each function is to each part of the general duty. As shown in paragraph 3.4, some functions may, by their nature, have little or no relevance.

3.13   A public authority should consider setting priorities, and giving priority to those functions that are most relevant to race equality.

Assessing impact and considering change

3.14   To assess the impact its functions and policies have on race equality, the authority may find it useful to draw up a clear statement of the aims of each function or policy. It should then consider whether it has information about how different racial groups are affected by the function or policy, as employees or users (or possible users) of services. The authority should also consider whether its functions and policies are promoting good race relations. The authority could get this information from various sources; for example previous research, records of complaints, surveys, or local meetings. These methods should help public authorities to assess which of their services are used by which racial groups, or what people think of their services, and whether they are being provided fairly to people from different racial groups. This kind of evidence should help public authorities to decide what they might need to do to meet all three parts of the general duty.

3.15   Public authorities may also need to consider adapting their existing information systems, so that they can provide information about different racial groups and show what progress the authority is making on race equality.

3.16   To assess the effects of a policy, or the way a function is being carried out, public authorities could ask themselves the following questions.

   a.   Could the policy or the way the function is carried out have an adverse impact on equality of opportunity for some racial groups? In other words, does it put some racial groups at a disadvantage?

   b.   Could the policy or the way the function is carried out have an adverse impact on relations between different racial groups?

   c.   Is the adverse impact, if any, unavoidable? Could it be considered to be unlawful racial discrimination? Can it be justified by the aims and importance of the policy or function? Are there other ways in which the authority's aims can be achieved without causing an adverse impact on some racial groups?

   d.   Could the adverse impact be reduced by taking particular measures?

   e.   Is further research or consultation necessary? Would this research be proportionate to the importance of the policy or function? Is it likely to lead to a different outcome?

3.17   If the assessment suggests that the policy, or the way the function is carried out, should be modified, the authority should do this to meet the general duty.

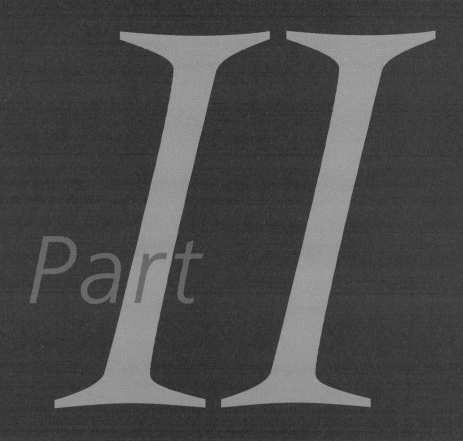

Part II

Promoting race equality in listed public authorities other than educational institutions

Public authorities – duties under the Race Relations Act

	Bound by the general duty APPENDIX 1	Bound by the duty to publish a race equality scheme APPENDIX 2	Bound by the employment duty APPENDIX 3	Bound by the duties for schools and further and higher education institutions APPENDIX 4
Government departments, local government, police, health, regulatory bodies, advice agencies, and commissions	✓	✓	✓	
Non-departmental public bodies (NDPBs), e.g. research councils, other agencies and commissions	✓		✓	
Advisory committees and councils, parish councils, and Welsh community councils	✓			
Governing bodies of schools	✓			✓
Governing bodies of further and higher education institutions	✓			✓

Promoting race equality
Specific duties: policy and service delivery

Relationship between the general and the specific duties

4.1 The specific duties have been introduced to help public authorities to meet the general duty. The specific duties are a means to an end – in other words, steps, methods or arrangements – rather than an end in themselves. Meeting the general duty is the main objective. This means that each time a public authority tackles a specific duty, it must consider whether it is meeting the three parts of the general duty (see 3.8). The authority needs regularly to ask this key question:

> What action should we take to:
> a. eliminate unlawful discrimination;
> b. promote equality of opportunity; and
> c. promote good race relations?

Race equality scheme

4.2 This chapter explains what arrangements the public authorities listed in appendix 2 must set out and publish as part of a race equality scheme. The arrangements in the scheme are not ends in themselves, but the necessary basic means for meeting the general duty. Some public authorities will already have made good progress towards putting these arrangements in place in carrying out some of their functions. Others may wish to go beyond the necessary minimum.

4.3 The necessary arrangements may not have to be new. Most of the main public services already have systems in place to meet their statutory requirements to collect information on performance, or to have their policies and services examined by independent inspection or audit agencies.

4.4 By publishing a race equality scheme, the public authority is accountable for its proposals for meeting the duty. This is also an opportunity for the authority to explain the values, principles and standards that guide its approach to race equality.

4.5   Under the specific duties, which came into effect on 3 December 2001, the listed public authorities had to publish a race equality scheme by **31 May 2002**. The scheme is a timetabled and realistic plan, setting out the authority's arrangements for meeting the general and specific duties.

4.6   The scheme should show how the public authority plans to meet its statutory duties under section 71(1) of the Race Relations Act (the Act) and, in particular, articles 2(2) and 2(3) of the Race Relations Act 1976 (Statutory Duties) Order 2001.

> 2. (2)   A Race Equality Scheme shall state, in particular –
>
> (a)   those of its functions and policies, or proposed policies, which that person has assessed as relevant to its performance of the duty imposed by section 71(1) of the Race Relations Act; and
>
> (b)   that person's arrangements for –
>
> (i)   assessing and consulting on the likely impact of its proposed policies on the promotion of race equality;
>
> (ii)   monitoring its policies for any adverse impact on the promotion of race equality;
>
> (iii)   publishing the results of such assessments and consultation as are mentioned in sub-paragraph (i) and of such monitoring as is mentioned in sub-paragraph (ii);
>
> (iv)   ensuring public access to information and services which it provides; and
>
> (v)   training staff in connection with the duties imposed by section 71(1) of the Race Relations Act and this Order.
>
> (3)   Such a person shall, within a period of three years from 31st May 2002, and within each further period of three years, review the assessment referred to in paragraph (2)(a).

4.7   All public authorities that have to publish a race equality scheme also have specific employment duties, which are explained in chapter 5. These authorities may find it useful to include the arrangements they make to meet their employment duties in their race equality schemes.

4.8   The race equality scheme can be part of a more general equality strategy or improvement plan, as long as it can be easily identified as meeting all the statutory requirements for this type of scheme.

Identifying relevant functions and policies

4.9 **Public authorities must list in their race equality scheme the functions and policies (including their proposed policies) that are relevant to the general duty to promote race equality. They should review this list at least every three years (see 4.6).**

4.10 The general principles for identifying functions have already been described under the general duty (see 3.4). To decide whether a function or policy is relevant to the general duty to promote race equality, public authorities should consider whether that function or policy could affect different racial groups in different ways or affect good race relations. (See the glossary for definitions of 'functions' and 'policies'.)

4.11 To make sure they meet the duty, for each function or policy, public authorities might ask:

   a. whether, and how, each of the three parts of the general duty – eliminating discrimination, promoting equality of opportunity, and promoting good race relations – applies;

   b. which racial groups are affected; and

   c. whether there is any reason to believe that people are, or could be, differently affected because of their racial group.

4.12 Public authorities will find it useful to make a list of all their functions, and to assess the relevance of these functions to the duty to promote race equality. In some cases, the assessment will need to consider the relevance and effect of particular policies.

4.13 If the authority is not sure how a particular function or policy might affect race equality, it could consider that function or policy as potentially relevant from the start. The authority should also consider new functions or policies whose effects have not yet been assessed in a similar way.

4.14 In practice, authorities will want to know how relevant each function or policy is to the general duty. They can then give it appropriate priority. For each function or policy, they might ask:

   a. whether there is already evidence that the function or policy is affecting some racial groups differently;

   b. whether there is any public concern that the function or policy in question is causing discrimination; and

   c. whether there is any public concern that the function or policy is damaging good race relations.

4.15 Listing functions in order of priority can help public authorities to organise and plan their action. However, to meet the terms of the Act they will need to look at all relevant functions and policies. The race equality scheme should allow for this review.

Arrangements for assessing, and consulting on, the likely impact of proposed policies

4.16 **Public authorities must set out in their race equality scheme their arrangements for assessing, and consulting on, the likely impact of their proposed policies on race equality (see 4.6).**

4.17 Public authorities are expected to set out their arrangements for:

a. assessing the likely impact their proposed policies will have, including their arrangements for collecting data;

b. consulting groups that may be affected by the policies.

4.18 Public authorities may find that they can use the arrangements they already have in place to carry out the necessary assessments and consultations.

Assessment

4.19 Assessing the likely impact of a proposed policy should help to identify whether that policy might have a different impact on some racial groups, and whether it will contribute to good race relations. The assessment may involve using:

a. information that is already available;

b. research findings;

c. population data, including census findings;

d. comparisons with similar policies in other authorities;

e. survey results;

f. ethnic data collected at different stages of a process (for example, when people apply for a service);

g. one-off data-gathering exercises; or

h. specially-commissioned research.

Consultation

4.20 Public authorities already consult people in a number of different ways. However, an authority will raise confidence in its services and improve the way it develops policy if it uses clear consultation methods and explains them to its staff and to the public.

4.21 Public authorities could consult people through:

   a. consultation meetings;

   b. focus groups;

   c. reference groups;

   d. citizens' juries;

   e. public scrutiny; or

   f. survey questionnaires.

4.22 Whichever consultation method they use, public authorities should try to make sure that:

   a. they use people's views to shape their decision-making process;

   b. the exercise represents the views of those who are likely to be affected by the policy;

   c. the consultation method is suitable for both the topic and the groups involved;

   d. the exercise is in proportion to the effect that the policy is likely to have;

   e. the consultation's aims are clearly explained;

   f. the consultation exercise is properly timetabled;

   g. the consultation exercise is monitored; and

   h. the consultation's findings are published.

4.23 If the assessment or consultation shows that the proposed policy is likely to have an adverse impact or harm race equality, the public authority will want to consider how it is going to meet the general duty to promote race equality. The authority might ask itself the following questions.

   a. If one of our policies leads to unlawful racial discrimination, can we find another way of meeting our aims?

   b. If one of our policies adversely affects people from certain racial groups, can we justify it because of its overall objectives? If we adapt the policy, could that compensate for any adverse effects?

c. If the assessment or consultation exercise reveals that certain racial groups have different needs, can we meet these needs, either within the proposed policy or in some other way?

d. Could the policy harm good race relations?

e. Will changes to the policy be significant, and will we need fresh consultation?

Arrangements for monitoring policies for adverse impact

4.24 **Public authorities must set out in their race equality scheme their arrangements for monitoring their policies for any adverse impact on race equality (see 4.6).**

4.25 Knowing that a policy is working as it should is vital to achieving the aims of the general duty. Keeping track of how a policy is working, and whether it is having an adverse impact or harming race equality, depends largely on having an efficient, up-to-date, and relevant monitoring system.

4.26 Under this duty, public authorities should set out their arrangements to monitor all the policies that are relevant to the general duty to promote race equality. These could include a wide range of policies, such as service delivery, as well as regulatory and enforcement functions, such as licensing or 'stop and search'.

4.27 Monitoring allows public authorities to test:

a. how racial groups are affected by their policies (for example, how often and why people use a service, how often they experience enforcement or legal action, how often they make complaints and why, and whether they face disadvantage or find that their needs are not met);

b. whether people from all groups are equally satisfied with the way they are treated;

c. whether services are provided effectively to all communities; and

d. whether services are suitable and designed to meet different needs (for example, whether they recognise language difficulties, individual cultural needs, or long-standing patterns of discrimination or exclusion).

4.28 Arrangements that the authority makes, or changes, to meet the duty should be relevant to the size of the authority, the nature of the policy and its possible effect on the public, particularly on different racial groups. Authorities can use a range of methods to monitor and analyse the effects of their policies on different racial groups, including:

a. statistical analysis of ethnic monitoring data;

b. satisfaction surveys (analysed by the racial groups to which the people surveyed belong);

c. random or targeted surveys; and

d. meetings, focus groups, and citizens' juries.

4.29 A public authority's arrangements might explain what it would do if its monitoring showed that one of its policies was having an adverse impact on race equality, and that it would prevent the authority from meeting its general duty.

4.30 The authority should ask the following questions.

a. If one of our policies is leading to unlawful racial discrimination, can we find another way to meet our aims?

b. If one of our policies is adversely affecting people from certain racial groups, can we justify the policy because of its overall objectives? If we adapt the policy, could that compensate for any adverse effects?

c. If the policy is harming good race relations, what should we do?

d. Will changes to the policy be significant, and will we need to consult about them?

Arrangements for publishing assessment, consultation and monitoring reports

4.31 **Public authorities must set out in their race equality scheme their arrangements for publishing the results of any assessments, consultations and monitoring they carry out to see whether their policies have an adverse impact on race equality (see 4.6).**

4.32 Publishing these results will increase an authority's openness and allow it to show that it is committed to promoting race equality. In time, this should increase public confidence in the authority – across all racial groups.

4.33 An authority's publishing arrangements should be in proportion to its size and the importance of the subject.

4.34 The authority should arrange to include the following points in publishing the results of consultations:

a. why the consultation took place;

b. how it was carried out;

    c.   a summary of the responses or views it produced;

    d.   an assessment of the policy options; and

    e.   what the public authority is proposing to do.

4.35   The authority should set out in its race equality scheme how often, and in what form, the results of its assessments, consultations and monitoring will be published. The authority's publishing arrangements might also take account of how these fit in with its other statutory requirements or demands for published information.

Arrangements for making sure the public have access to information and services

4.36   **Public authorities must set out in their race equality scheme their arrangements for making sure that the public have access to information and services they provide (see 4.6).**

4.37   To meet this specific duty, public authorities should arrange to make their information and services accessible to everyone. Authorities might consider the following.

    a.   Consider access to information and services when they assess their functions. For example, is there enough information available to the public? Is the information user-friendly?

    b.   Consider whether a service is not being fully used because people do not have enough information about it, or because they are not confident that the service can meet their particular needs sympathetically or fairly.

    c.   Ask whether information is available at the right time and in the right place.

    d.   Take steps to improve the information available.

    e.   Monitor how effectively information is given to the public, and make improvements, where necessary.

    f.   Make sure that staff have the skills, information and understanding needed to deal fairly and equally with all clients.

4.38   Public authorities might also consider how they can improve public access to their services. Possible ways include:

    a.   asking local communities what services they need and how they want them provided;

    b.   providing 'outreach' services to particular groups in an environment and style they are familiar with;

c. strengthening cooperation with particular groups;

d. arranging for interpreters;

e. taking positive action (see the glossary); and

f. developing access to computers and internet services.

Arrangements for training staff

4.39 **Public authorities must set out in their race equality scheme their arrangements for training their staff in connection with the general duty to promote race equality, and any specific duties (see 4.6).**

4.40 Staff-training arrangements under this duty should aim to make sure that staff responsible for meeting the general and specific duties are aware of these – and have the skills needed to carry them out. Public authorities should consider what staff at various levels need to know about the general and specific duties, before giving them the training they need. This specific duty also includes meeting the training needs of the staff responsible for managing and delivering the public authority's race equality scheme. Staff training should therefore focus on what the authority needs to do to meet the duties laid down in the Race Relations Act and any specific duties.

5

Promoting race equality
Specific duties: employment

5.1 The specific duty on employment applies to most of the public authorities bound by the general duty (see appendix 3). Schools and further and higher education institutions are not bound by the employment duty, as they have separate employment responsibilities (see chapter 6). A few, mainly advisory, agencies are also not bound by the employment duty.

5.2 Articles 5(1), 5(2), and 5(3) of the Race Relations Act 1976 (Statutory Duties) Order 2001 say the following:

> 5. (1) *A person to which this article applies shall,*
>
> (a) *before 31st May 2002, have in place arrangements for fulfilling, as soon as is reasonably practicable, its duties under paragraph (2); and*
>
> (b) *fulfil those duties in accordance with such arrangements.*
>
> (2) *It shall be the duty of such a person to monitor, by reference to the racial groups to which they belong,*
>
> (a) *the numbers of –*
>
> (i) *staff in post, and*
>
> (ii) *applicants for employment, training and promotion, from each such group, and*
>
> (b) *where that person has 150 or more full-time staff, the numbers of staff from each such group who -*
>
> (i) *receive training;*
>
> (ii) *benefit or suffer detriment as a result of its performance assessment procedures;*
>
> (iii) *are involved in grievance procedures;*
>
> (iv) *are the subject of disciplinary procedures; or*
>
> (v) *cease employment with that person.*
>
> (3) *Such a person shall publish annually the results of its monitoring under paragraph (2).*

Part *IV*

Role of the
Commission for
Racial Equality

5.3   Public authorities that have to produce race equality schemes may find it useful to include their arrangements for meeting their employment duty in their race equality schemes.

5.4   The specific duties on employment are designed to provide a framework for measuring progress in equality of opportunity in public-sector employment. The specific duties are also aimed at providing monitoring information to guide initiatives that could lead to a more representative public-sector workforce. For example, these initiatives could include setting recruitment targets for under-represented racial groups, or targeting management development courses at racial groups that are under-represented at certain levels. The specific duties on employment set minimum standards. Other issues may also be relevant for good employment practice. This will depend on local circumstances.

5.5   Ethnic monitoring (see the glossary) is central to providing a clear picture of what is happening during the authority's employment cycle – from applying for a job and joining the authority to leaving it. Monitoring helps to measure overall progress and to show whether the authority's equal opportunities policies are effective. Monitoring is the essential tool to assess progress – or lack of it – in removing barriers to equality of opportunity in the public services.

5.6   It is important that the authority explains to applicants and existing staff why they are monitoring employment. People will normally only have to give information about their racial group voluntarily, and the authority should explain the conditions of the Data Protection Act 1998 (about processing this information) to them.

5.7   Wherever possible, the authority should build monitoring information into the information systems it already uses. The authority may be able to publish its monitoring results each year through its existing reporting systems. In its published results, the authority should explain how it is dealing with trends or problems highlighted by its monitoring. The authority may also find it useful to combine and analyse ethnic monitoring data with other data; for example on sex and disability.

5.8   To help meet the specific duty on employment, public authorities should:

a.   collect ethnic monitoring data; and

b.   publish the results of the monitoring each year.

5.9   To check that they are meeting the general duty, public authorities may want to:

a.   analyse the data to find any patterns of inequality; and

b.   take whatever steps are needed to remove barriers and promote equality of opportunity.

5.10 If the monitoring shows that current employment policies, procedures and practice are leading to unlawful racial discrimination, the authority should take steps to end the discrimination. As a first step, the authority should examine each of its procedures closely to find out where and how discrimination might be happening, and then consider what changes to introduce.

5.11 On the other hand, the monitoring may show that current policies, procedures and practice have an adverse impact on equality of opportunity or good race relations (even though they are not causing unlawful discrimination). If this is the case, the authority should consider changing its policies or procedures so that they still meet the same aims, but do not harm equality of opportunity or race relations.

Positive action

5.12 If monitoring reveals that some racial groups are under-represented in the workforce, the authority could consider using 'positive action' (see the glossary). This allows employers and others to target their job training and recruitment efforts at those groups that are under-represented in a particular area of work. However, positive action does not allow discrimination when deciding who will be offered a job.

Ethnic categories and the 2001 census

5.13 Public authorities are encouraged to use the same ethnic classification system as the one used in the 2001 census. Some authorities already have systems in place. If an authority chooses to collect more detailed information, it should make sure that the categories are the same as, or similar to, those used in the 2001 census. Any extra ethnic categories it adds to reflect its particular circumstances should fit in with the 2001 census categories.

5.14 Public authorities should make realistic and timetabled plans to adapt their ethnic monitoring systems to meet the specific duties.

5.15 The 2001 census used different ethnic classifications for England and Wales, and Scotland.

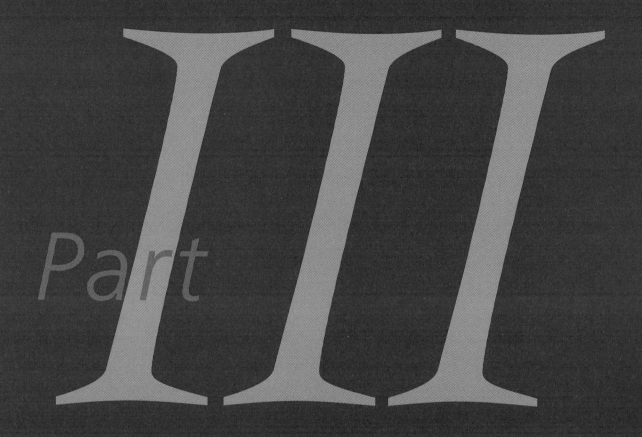

Part III

Promoting race equality in educational institutions

6

Promoting race equality
Specific duties: educational institutions

Introduction

6.1 This part of the code is written mainly for education providers. They are as follows.

    a. The governing bodies of maintained schools (see the glossary) and other educational institutions maintained by a local education authority (LEA) – in other words, all community, foundation and voluntary schools, and special schools maintained by the LEA.

    b. The governing bodies of City Technology Colleges, City Colleges for Technology or the Arts, and City Academies.

    c. The governing bodies of further education institutions (see the glossary).

    d. The governing bodies of higher education institutions (see the glossary).

6.2 Schools and further and higher education institutions must all meet the general duty. Chapter 3 explains what they need to do to meet the duty. The Home Secretary has also placed specific duties on schools (see 6.7 – 6.22), and on further and higher education institutions (see 6.23 – 6.44), to help them to meet the general duty.

6.3 The specific duties on employment, described in chapter 5, do not apply directly to schools. The main responsibility for monitoring employment rests with LEAs. All schools are expected to give their LEA ethnic monitoring data on their staff from their regular returns, so that the LEA can meet the duty.

6.4 Further and higher education institutions have other employment duties, which are described in paragraphs 6.39 to 6.41. As well as these duties, further and higher education institutions will have to give bodies such as the higher education funding councils (see 6.45 – 6.48 for details of the specific duties placed on these bodies), monitoring information about their teaching staff.

6.5 The aim of the general duty is to make race equality central to the way public authorities carry out their functions (see the glossary). Promoting race equality should be a central part of all policy development, service delivery and employment practice.

Benefits of the duty

6.6   Meeting the duty will help the educational institution to do the following.

a.   Make sure that the needs of all pupils and students are met and that they are able to achieve their full potential. The duty will help to raise standards across the whole institution.

b.   Target action (including resources and support) to remove inequalities between racial groups in their levels of achievement and progress; their experience of disciplinary measures (such as exclusion); admissions; or assessment.

c.   Create a positive atmosphere where there is a shared commitment to value diversity and respect difference.

d.   Challenge and prevent racism and discrimination, and promote good relations between people from different racial groups.

e.   Prepare pupils and students to be good citizens, living and working in a multi-ethnic society.

f.   Create and retain a workforce that represents different ethnic backgrounds.

g.   Attract a motivated and loyal workforce, where employees from all racial groups are valued and can reach their full potential.

h.   Make full use of the skills and different perspectives in the community when running the institution (for example, as governors or board members), delivering the curriculum, and supporting pupils, students and staff.

Schools

6.7   Articles 3(1), 3(2), 3(3), and 3(5) of the Race Relations Act 1976 (Statutory Duties) Order 2001 place specific duties on governing bodies of schools (see the glossary). Such a body shall:

3. (1) .... before 31st May 2002,

(a)   prepare a written statement of its policy for promoting race equality (referred to in this article as its "race equality policy"), and

(b)   have in place arrangements for fulfilling, as soon as is reasonably practicable, its duties under paragraph (3)...

(2) Such a body shall,

(a)   maintain a copy of the statement, and

(b)   fulfil those duties in accordance with such arrangements.

(3) It shall be the duty of [such] a body ... to –

> (a) assess the impact of its policies, including its race equality policy, on pupils, staff and parents of different racial groups including, in particular, the impact on attainment levels of such pupils; and
>
> (b) monitor, by reference to their impact on such pupils, staff and parents, the operation of such policies including, in particular, their impact on the attainment levels of such pupils.
>
> .....
>
> (5) Such a body shall take such steps as are reasonably practicable to publish annually the results of its monitoring under this article.

Race equality policy

6.8 **Schools must prepare and maintain a written statement of their race equality policy, and have arrangements in place for meeting their duties as soon as reasonably possible. Both the statement and arrangements had to be ready by 31 May 2002 (see 6.7).**

6.9 A race equality policy will help the school to prevent racial discrimination, and to promote equality of opportunity and good race relations across all areas of school activity. The policy should be part of the planning arrangements the school already makes.

6.10 The race equality policy should be a written statement of responsibilities and commitments. It could be linked to an action plan for putting the policy into practice. A good policy would:

a. be part of the school's development plan;

b. give details of how the school will put the policy into practice and assess how effective it is;

c. clearly define roles and responsibilities, so that people know what is expected of them; and

d. explain clearly what the school will do if the policy is not followed.

6.11 The race equality policy can be combined with another policy, such as an equal opportunities or diversity policy. However, to meet this duty, the race equality policy should be clearly identifiable and easily available.

6.12 The race equality policy should reflect the character and circumstances of the school, and deal with the main areas that are relevant to promoting the general duty. For example:

a. pupils' attainment and progress;

b. curriculum, teaching and learning (including language and cultural needs);

    c.   promoting good race relations in the school and in the local community;

    d.   care and assessment;

    e.   staff recruitment and career development;

    f.   the school's values;

    g.   pupil behaviour, discipline and exclusion;

    h.   racial harassment and bullying;

    i.   admission and transfer procedures;

    j.   membership of the governing body;

    k.   involving parents and the community in the school.

Assessing the impact of policies

6.13 **Under the duty, schools must assess the impact their policies (including their race equality policy) have on pupils, staff and parents from different racial groups. In particular, schools should assess whether their policies have, or could have, an adverse impact on the attainment levels of pupils from different racial groups (see 6.7).**

6.14 The school should assess how effective its race equality policy is through the arrangements it has already made to develop and review policies.

Assessing impact on pupils, staff and parents

6.15 The main questions for assessing the impact of a school's policies, including its race equality policy – giving special attention to pupils' attainment levels – could include the following.

    a.   Is the school making sure that its policies, for example on exclusion, bullying, the curriculum, parental involvement, community involvement, and race equality, are not having an adverse impact on pupils, staff or parents from some racial groups?

    b.   How does the school help all staff to develop and reach their full potential?

    c.   How does the school encourage all parents to take part fully in the life of the school?

    d.   Does the school help all its pupils to achieve as much as they can, and get the most from what is on offer, based on their individual needs?

    e.   How does the school explain any differences? Are the explanations justified? Can they be justified on non-racial grounds, such as English language difficulties?

f.   Does each relevant policy include aims to deal with differences (or possible differences) in pupils' attainments between racial groups? Do the policy's aims lead to action to deal with any differences that have been identified (for example, extra coaching for pupils, or steps to prevent racist bullying)?

g.   What is the school doing to raise standards, and promote equality of opportunity for pupils who seem to be underachieving and who may need extra support?

h.   What is the school doing to:

(i)   prepare pupils for living in a multi-ethnic society;

(ii) promote race equality and harmony in the school, and in the local community; and

(iii) prevent or deal with racism?

i.   Is the action the school has taken appropriate and effective? Are there any unexpected results? If so, how are they being handled?

j.   What changes does the school need to make to relevant policies, policy aims, and any related targets and strategies?

6.16   To answer these questions, schools could consider:

a.   collecting and analysing relevant monitoring and other data;

b.   talking to pupils, parents and staff to find out their needs and opinions; and

c.   carrying out surveys or special research.

6.17   Schools could use the results of these assessments to:

a.   rethink their race equality objectives (where necessary); and

b.   influence and guide their planning and decision making.

Monitoring the impact of policies

6.18   **Under the duty, schools must monitor the impact of their policies on pupils, parents and staff from different racial groups. In particular, schools should monitor the impact of their policies on pupils' attainment levels (see 6.7).**

6.19   To monitor their pupils' attainment, schools collect information about pupils' performance and progress, by racial group. They will need to analyse the information, and use it to examine trends. To help interpret this information, schools may find it useful to examine other areas that could have an impact on pupils' attainment.

6.20   Monitoring information will help schools to see what progress they are making towards meeting their race equality targets and objectives. In particular, it will help them to:

a. highlight any differences in attainment between pupils from different racial groups;

b. ask why these differences exist, and test the explanations given;

c. review how effective their current targets and objectives are; and

d. decide what further action may be needed to meet the three parts of the general duty (see 1.1), and to improve the performance of pupils from different racial groups.

Publishing

6.21 **Under the duty, schools must take reasonably practicable steps to publish the results of its monitoring each year (see 6.7).**

6.22 The school should use the arrangements it already has in place to publish the results of the monitoring it carries out to meet the duty. Summaries of the results, highlighting trends and key issues and outlining the steps the school is planning to take, should be sufficient.

Further and higher education institutions

6.23 Articles 3(1), 3(2), 3(4), and 3(5) of the Race Relations Act 1976 (Statutory Duties) Order 2001 place specific duties on further and higher education institutions. Such a body shall:

>   3. (1) … before 31st May 2002,
>
>   (a) prepare a written statement of its policy for promoting race equality (referred to in this article as its "race equality policy"), and
>
>   (b) have in place arrangements for fulfilling, as soon as is reasonably practicable, its duties under paragraph … (4)….
>
>   (2) Such a body shall,
>
>   (a) maintain a copy of the statement, and
>
>   (b) fulfil those duties in accordance with such arrangements.
>
>   …
>
>   (4) It shall be the duty of [such] a body … to –
>
>   (a) assess the impact of its policies, including its race equality policy, on students and staff of different racial groups;

(b) *monitor, by reference to those racial groups, the admission and progress of students and the recruitment and career progress of staff; and*

(c) *include in its written statement of its race equality policy an indication of its arrangements for publishing that statement and the results of its assessment and monitoring under sub-paragraphs (a) and (b).*

(5) *Such a body shall take such steps as are reasonably practicable to publish annually the results of its monitoring under this article.*

Race equality policy

6.24 **Under the duty, further and higher education institutions must prepare and maintain a written statement of their race equality policy, and have arrangements in place for meeting their duties as soon as reasonably possible. Both the statement and arrangements must be ready by 31 May 2002 (see 6.23).**

6.25 A race equality policy will help the institution to prevent racial discrimination, and promote equality of opportunity and good race relations across all areas of activity. The policy should be part of the planning arrangements the institution already makes.

6.26 The race equality policy should be a written statement of responsibilities and commitments. It could be linked to an action plan for putting the policy into practice. A good policy would:

a. be part of the institution's yearly plan;

b. give details of how the institution will put the policy into practice, monitor it, and assess how effective it is;

c. provide a framework for building race equality into other relevant policies, and into all relevant areas of the institution's activities;

d. clearly define roles and responsibilities so that people know what is expected of them;

e. explain clearly what the institution will do if the policy is not followed; and

f. set out the institution's arrangements for publishing, each year, its race equality policy and the results of the monitoring and assessments it carries out to meet the duty.

6.27 The race equality policy should reflect the character and circumstances of the institution, and deal with the main areas that are relevant to promoting equality of opportunity and good race relations, and tackling racial discrimination. These areas may include:

a. the institution's values;

b. curriculum, teaching and learning (including language and cultural needs);

c. assessment;

d. racial harassment and bullying;

e. the institution's management and governing body;

f. admissions, access and participation;

g. student support and guidance;

h. behaviour and discipline;

i. partnerships and community links; and

j. staff recruitment, training and career development.

6.28   The race equality policy can be combined with another policy, such as an equal opportunities or diversity policy. However, to meet this duty, the race equality policy will need to be clearly identifiable and easily available.

Assessing the impact of policies

6.29   **Under the duty, further and higher education institutions must assess the impact of their policies (including the race equality policy) on students and staff from different racial groups (see 6.23).**

6.30   The purpose of the assessment is to see whether the institution's policies help to achieve race equality for students and staff from different racial groups or whether they have, or could have, an adverse impact on them.

6.31   The institution should assess the impact its policies have on students and staff from different racial groups. They may find it helpful to build this assessment into the arrangements they already have for reviewing their policies.

6.32   Questions for assessing the impact of the institution's policies could include the following.

a. Is the institution helping all staff and students to achieve as much as they can, and get as much as they can from what is provided for them?

b. How does the institution explain the differences between groups of students in terms of teaching and learning, drop-out rates, student progression and achievement, assessment, access to learning resources, support and guidance, and curricular and other opportunities?

c. Are these explanations justified? Can they be justified on non-racial grounds (for example, English language difficulties)?

d. How does the institution explain the differences between groups of staff in terms of grade and position, type of contract, career development, training, and other opportunities?

e. Are these explanations justified? Can they be justified on non-racial grounds (for example, a change in institution-wide policy on permanent recruitment)?

f. What is the institution doing to:

   (i)   raise achievement levels and tackle race inequalities when recruiting staff, and in students' performance and progress;

   (ii) promote race equality and harmony, both inside the institution and in the wider community; and

   (iii) prevent, or deal with, racism?

g. Do the policy's aims lead to action to deal with any unjustifiable differences that are identified?

h. Is the action appropriate and effective? Are there any unexpected results? If so, how are they being handled?

i. What changes does the institution need to make to policies, relevant policy aims, and related targets and strategies?

6.33 To answer these questions, further and higher institutions could consider:

a. collecting and analysing relevant monitoring and other information;

b. talking to staff and students from all racial groups to find out their needs and opinions; and

c. carrying out surveys and research studies.

6.34 Further and higher education institutions could use these assessments to:

a. rethink their race equality objectives (where necessary); and

b. influence and guide their planning and decision making.

Monitoring admission, recruitment and progress

6.35 **Under the duty, further and higher education institutions must monitor, by racial group, student admission and progress, and staff recruitment and career progress (see 6.23).**

6.36 Monitoring involves collecting information to measure an institution's perform-ance and effectiveness. The results may suggest how the institution can improve.

6.37 The institution should monitor all stages of the student admissions process, from applications to outcomes. To help interpret the information, the institution might also consider monitoring other areas that could have an adverse impact on students from some racial groups, such as:

a. choice of subject;

b. home or international status; and

c. selection methods.

6.38 The institution should monitor all students' achievements and progress. To help interpret the information, the institution might also consider monitoring other areas that could have an adverse impact on students from some racial groups, such as:

a. student numbers, transfers and drop-outs;

b. different methods of assessing students;

c. work placements;

d. the results of programmes targeted at people from specific racial groups; and

e. bullying and racial harassment.

6.39 The institution should monitor all activities that relate to staff recruitment and selection, and to career development and opportunities for promotion. It might consider monitoring for each department as well as the whole institution. This is likely to include:

a. selecting and training panel members;

b. applications and appointments;

c. success rates for the different selection methods;

d. permanent, temporary or fixed-term appointments; and

e. home or international status (for institutions that recruit internationally).

6.40 The institution should identify areas where career progress could be affected and monitor those. They might include:

a. staff, by their grade and type of post;

b. staff, by their length of service;

c. staff training and development, including applications and selection, if appropriate;

d. the results of training and career-development programmes or strategies that target staff from particular racial groups;

e. staff appraisals; and

f. staff promotion, including recruitment methods and criteria for choosing candidates.

6.41   The institution will find it useful to assess its monitoring information regularly. This will allow it to evaluate the progress it is making in meeting its race equality targets and aims. These assessments will help the institution to:

a.   highlight any differences between staff and students from different racial groups;

b.   ask why these differences exist;

c.   review how effective its current targets and aims are;

d.   decide what more it can do to improve the performance of students from different racial groups (including positive action as allowed in section 35 of the Race Relations Act; see the glossary) and to improve the recruitment and progression of staff from different racial groups (again including positive action as allowed in sections 37 and 38 of the Race Relations Act; see the glossary); and

e.   decide what further action it may need to take to meet the three parts of the general duty.

Publishing

6.42   **Under the duty, further and higher education institutions must include a statement in their written race equality policy about their arrangements for publishing the race equality policy, and the results of assessments and monitoring. The duty also requires institutions to take reasonably practicable steps to publish, each year, the results of the monitoring they carry out to meet the duty. (See 6.23.)**

6.43   The institution's race equality policy should explain what will be published, and the form in which the information will be published. The institution should use the arrangements it already has in place to publish the results of its monitoring and assessments.

6.44   The institution might also consider publishing the results of any consultations they carry out to meet the duty. The information they publish could include:

a.   why the consultation took place;

b.   how the consultation was carried out;

c.   a summary of the responses or views expressed;

d.   an assessment of the policy options; and

e.   what the institution is proposing to do.

Employment duties of bodies with specific responsibilities for education

6.45 Local education authorities (LEAs) have a duty to monitor by racial group, for all the maintained schools in their area, the following:

a. staff in post; and

b. applicants for employment, training and promotion;

c. for schools with 150 or more full-time staff, or equivalent, the number of staff:

(i) receiving training;

(ii) benefiting, or suffering a detriment, as a result of performance assessment procedures;

(iii) involved in grievance procedures;

(iv) subject to disciplinary procedures; and

(v) ending employment with these schools.

6.46 LEAs have a duty to take reasonably practicable steps to publish, each year, the results of this monitoring.

6.47 The Department for Education and Skills has a duty to:

a. monitor, by racial group, the number of teaching staff from each racial group at all maintained schools;

b. take reasonably practicable steps to use information provided by LEAs for that purpose; and

c. take reasonably practicable steps to publish, each year, the results of this monitoring.

6.48 The Learning and Skills Council for England, the Higher Education Funding Councils for England and Wales, and the National Council for Education and Training for Wales have a duty to:

a. monitor, by racial group, the number of teaching staff at all the establishments for which they are responsible; and

b. take reasonably practicable steps to publish, each year, the results of this monitoring.

7

Partnership and enforcement
Role of the Commission for Racial Equality

7.1 The Commission for Racial Equality (CRE) was set up under the Race Relations Act as an independent statutory agency. The CRE reports every year to the Home Secretary, but it is not formally part of the Home Office. The duties of the CRE, as set out in the Act, are to:

a. work towards eliminating discrimination;

b. promote equality of opportunity and good relations between persons of different racial groups; and

c. review the workings of the Act.

7.2 The CRE has both promotional and enforcement powers, and both apply to its work on the duty to promote race equality. This chapter explains how the CRE will use both these powers to help promote race equality.

Partnership

Helping public authorities to meet their duty

7.3 The CRE will:

a. give practical advice;

b. work with main parts of the public sector, including the inspectorates, to develop good practice; and

c. monitor and spread good practice.

Providing practical guidance

7.4 The CRE has issued non-statutory supplementary guides to this code, for public authorities, schools and further and higher education institutions (see appendix 6).

7.5 The CRE will continue to work with public authorities to help them to meet their general and specific duties.

Developing and monitoring good practice

7.6 The CRE works with public authorities to develop and share good practice in a number of ways, for example by:

   a. sharing and demonstrating good practice;

   b. supporting training;

   c. giving information and advice;

   d. updating guidance and publishing other material;

   e. promoting good practice; and

   f. identifying poor practice.

Enforcement

7.7 The CRE is committed to using the full range of its enforcement powers appropriately. The CRE has a new power under the Act to enforce the specific duties to promote race equality.

The general duty

7.8 If a public authority does not meet the general duty, its actions (or failure to act) can be challenged by a claim to the High Court for judicial review (see the glossary). A claim for judicial review can be made by a person or group of people with an interest in the matter, or by the CRE.

Specific duties

7.9 If a public authority does not meet any of its specific duties, it could face enforcement action by the CRE under section 71D of the Race Relations Act.

7.10 If the CRE is satisfied that a public authority has failed (or is failing) to meet any of its specific duties, the CRE can serve a 'compliance notice' on that authority. This notice will state that the authority must meet its duty and tell the CRE, within 28 days, what it has done, or is doing, to meet its duty.

7.11 In the compliance notice, the CRE can also ask the authority to give it written information showing that it has met its duty. The notice will state the time by which the CRE should receive the information. The CRE cannot ask for more information than a public authority would have to provide during High Court proceedings in England, or in the Scottish Court of Sessions.

7.12 If, three months after a compliance notice has been served, the CRE considers that the authority has still not met one or more of its specific duties referred to in the notice, the CRE can apply to the county court (in England) or sheriff court (in Scotland) for an order to obey the notice.

7.13　If the compliance notice says that the authority must provide information, and it has not done so within the given time – or the CRE believes that the authority will not provide the information – the CRE can apply to the county court (in England) or sheriff court (in Scotland) for an order saying that the authority must provide the relevant information.

7.14　The county court or sheriff court may grant the order in the terms that the CRE applied for, or in more limited terms. If the court makes an order and the authority does not keep to it, the authority may be found in contempt of court.

Unlawful discrimination

7.15　The Act gives individuals the right to take legal action against unlawful racial discrimination. The Act also gives the CRE the power to take legal action against certain acts of unlawful discrimination. This power includes the power to carry out formal investigations (see the glossary).

CRE codes of practice

7.16　This and other statutory codes of practice that the CRE issues under the Act are admissible in evidence in court. A court will be expected to take the code of practice into account if it seems relevant to any matter the court is ruling on. Public authorities do not have to follow the guidance in this code of practice. However, they are expected to meet the general duty and any specific duties by which they are bound.

Part

V

Appendices

Appendix 1

Public authorities bound by the general duty

(SCHEDULE 1A OF THE RACE RELATIONS ACT 1976)

Ministers of the Crown and government departments

(1) A Minister of the Crown or government department
(2) Sub-paragraph (1) does not include the Security Service, the Intelligence Service or the Government Communications Headquarters

Scottish Administration

(1) An office-holder in the Scottish Administration (within the meaning given by section 126(7)(a) of the Scotland Act 1998)
(2) Members of the staff of the Scottish Administration (within the meaning given by section 126(7)(b) of that Act)

National Assembly for Wales

(1) The National Assembly for Wales
(2) An Assembly subsidiary as defined by section 99(4) of the Government of Wales Act 1998

Armed Forces

Any of the naval, military or air forces of the Crown

National Health Service: England and Wales

A Health Authority established under section 8 of the National Health Service Act 1977

A National Health Service trust established under section 5 of the National Health Service and Community Care Act 1990

A primary care trust established under section 16A of that Act

A special health authority established under section 11 of that Act

National Health Service: Scotland

A health board constituted under section 2 of the National Health Service (Scotland) Act 1978

A National Health Service trust established under section 12A of that Act

A special health board constituted under section 2 of that Act

Local government

A body corporate established pursuant to an order under section 67 of the Local Government Act 1985 (transfer of functions to successors of residuary bodies, etc)

A body corporate established pursuant to an order under section 22 of the Local Government Act 1992 (residuary bodies)

The Broads Authority established by section 1 of the Norfolk and Suffolk Broads Act 1988

Any charter trustees constituted under section 246 of that Act

The Common Council of the City of London in its capacity as a local authority or port health authority

A community council established under section 51 of the Local Government (Scotland) Act 1973

A council constituted under section 2 of the Local Government etc (Scotland) Act 1994

The Council of the Isles of Scilly

A fire authority constituted by a combination scheme under section 5 or 6 of the Fire Services Act 1947

The Greater London Authority

An internal drainage board which is continued in being by virtue of section 1 of the Land Drainage Act 1991

A joint authority established under Part IV of the Local Government Act 1985 (fire services, civil defence and transport)

A joint authority established under section 21 of the Local Government Act 1992

A joint board which is continued in being by virtue of section 263(1) of that Act

A joint board within the meaning of section 235(1) of the Local Government (Scotland) Act 1973

A joint committee constituted in accordance with section 102(1)(b) of the Local Government Act 1972

A joint planning board constituted for an area in Wales outside a National Park by an order under section 2(1B) of the Town and Country Planning Act 1990

A licensing board constituted under section 1 of the Licensing (Scotland) Act 1976

A local authority (within the meaning of the Local Government Act 1972), namely
(a) in England, a county council, a London borough council, a district council or a parish council;
(b) in Wales, a county council, a county borough council or a community council

A local probation board established under section 4 of the Criminal Justice and Court Services Act 2000

The London Development Agency

The London Fire and Emergency Planning Authority

A magistrates' courts committee established under section 27 of the Justices of the Peace Act 1997

A national park authority established by an order under section 63 of the Environment Act 1995

A parish meeting constituted under section 13 of the Local Government Act 1972

A passenger transport executive for a passenger transport area within the meaning of Part II of the Transport Act 1968

A port health authority constituted by an order under section 2 of the Public Health (Control of Disease) Act 1984

A regional development agency established under the Regional Development Agencies Act 1998 (other than the London Development Agency)

Scottish Enterprise and Highland and Islands Enterprise, established under the Enterprise and New Towns (Scotland) Act 1990

The Sub-Treasurer of the Inner Temple or the Under-Treasurer of the Middle Temple, in his capacity as a local authority

Transport for London

A waste disposal authority established by virtue of an order under section 10(1) of the Local Government Act 1985

The London Development Agency

Education

The Adult Learning Inspectorate

The board of management of a self governing school (within the meaning of the Self-Governing Schools etc (Scotland) Act 1992)

The board of management of a self-governing school (within the meaning of the Self-Governing Schools etc (Scotland) Act 1989)

The British Educational Communication and Technology Agency

A city academy established by an agreement under section 482 of the Education Act 1996

A city college for the technology of the arts established by an agreement under section 482 of the Education Act 1996

A city technology college established by an agreement under section 482 of the Education Act 1996

A college of further education maintained by an education authority, in the exercise of its further education functions in providing courses of further education (within the meaning of section 1(5)(b)(ii) of the Education (Scotland) Act 1980)

Community Learning Scotland

The Construction Industry Training Board

The Engineering Construction Industry Training Board

The General Teaching Council for England

The General Teaching Council for Scotland

The General Teaching Council for Wales

The governing body of an institution within the higher education sector (within the meaning of Part II of the Further and Higher Education (Scotland) Act 1992)

Governing bodies of –
(a) educational establishments maintained by local education authorities;
(b) institutions within the further education sector (within the meaning of section 91(3) of the Further and Higher Education Act 1992);
(c) institutions within the higher education sector (within the meaning of section 91(5) of the Act of 1992)

The Higher Education Funding Council for England

The Higher Education Funding Council for Wales

The Learning and Skills Council for England

Learning and Teaching Scotland

The managers of a central institution (within the meaning of section 135 of the Act of 1980)

The managers of a grant-aided school (within the meaning of section 135 of the Education (Scotland) Act 1980)

The National Council for Education and Training for Wales

Newbattle Abbey College

The Qualifications and Curriculum Authority

The Qualifications, Curriculum and Assessment Authority for Wales

The Quality Assurance Agency for Higher Education

Sabhal Mòr Ostaig College

The School Teachers' Review Body

The Scottish Further Education Funding Council

The Scottish Further Education Unit, in respect of its public functions

The Scottish Higher Education Funding Council

The Scottish Qualifications Authority

The Student Loans Company

The Teacher Training Agency

Housing bodies

A housing action trust established under Part III of the Housing Act 1988

The Housing Corporation

Scottish Homes

Police

The British Transport Police

A chief constable of a police force maintained under section 1 of the Police (Scotland) Act 1967

A chief constable of a police force maintained under section 2 of the Police Act 1996

The Chief Constable for the Ministry of Defence Police appointed by the Secretary of State under section 1(3) of the Ministry of Defence Police Act 1987

The Commissioner of Police for the City of London

The Commissioner of Police of the Metropolis

The Common Council of the City of London in its capacity as a police authority

The Metropolitan Police Authority established under section 5B of the Police Act 1996

A police authority established under section 2 of the Police (Scotland) Act 1967

A police authority established under section 3 of the Police Act 1996

The Police Complaints Authority

The Police Information Technology Organisation

The Police Negotiating Board

A selection panel for independent members of police authorities

The Service Authority for the National Crime Squad

The Service Authority for the National Criminal Intelligence Service

Health

The Administration of Radioactive Substances Advisory Committee

The Commission for Health Improvement

The Common Services Agency for the NHS in Scotland

The Council for Professions Supplementary to Medicine, in respect of its public functions

The Dental Practice Board

The English National Board for Nursing, Midwifery and Health Visiting

The Human Fertilisation and Embryology Authority

The Joint Committee on Postgraduate Training for General Practice

The Joint Committee on Vaccination and Immunisation

The Mental Welfare Commission for Scotland

The National Biological Standards Board

The Public Health Laboratory Service Board

The Royal College of Anaesthetists, in respect of its public functions

The Royal College of General Practitioners, in respect of its public functions

The Royal College of Midwives, in respect of its public functions

The Royal College of Nursing, in respect of its public functions

The Royal College of Obstetricians and Gynaecologists, in respect of its public functions

The Royal College of Ophthalmologists, in respect of its public functions

The Royal College of Paediatrics and Child Health, in respect of its public functions

The Royal College of Pathologists, in respect of its public functions

The Royal College of Physicians, in respect of its public functions

The Royal College of Psychiatrists, in respect of its public functions

The Royal College of Radiologists, in respect of its public functions

The Royal College of Speech and Language Therapists, in respect of its public functions

The Royal College of Surgeons of England, in respect of its public functions

The Scottish Dental Practice Board

The Scottish Hospital Endowments Research Trust

The Scottish Hospital Trust

The Scottish Medical Practices Committee

The Specialist Training Authority of the Medical Royal Colleges

The Standing Dental Advisory Committee

The Standing Medical Advisory Committee

The Standing Nursing and Midwifery Advisory Committee

The Standing Pharmaceutical Advisory Committee

The Unrelated Live Transplant Regulatory Authority

The Welsh Committee for Professional Development of Pharmacy

The Welsh Dental Committee

The Welsh Medical Committee

The Welsh National Board for Nursing, Midwifery and Health Visiting

The Welsh Nursing and Midwifery Committee

The Welsh Optometric Committee

The Welsh Pharmaceutical Committee

Libraries, museums and arts

The Advisory Committee on Sites of Special Scientific Interest

The Advisory Council on Public Records

The Ancient Monuments Board for Scotland

The Ancient Monuments Board for Wales

The Arts Council of England

The Arts Council of Wales

The British Library

The British Museum

The British Tourist Authority

The Commission for Architecture and the Built Environment

The Countryside Council for Wales

The Design Council

English Nature

The English Tourist Board

The Film Council

The Geffrye Museum

The Historic Buildings and Monuments Commission for England

The Historic Buildings Council for Scotland

The Historic Buildings Council for Wales

The Historic Royal Palaces Trust

The Horniman Museum

The Imperial War Museum

The Library and Information Services Council (Wales)

The Millennium Commission

The Museum of London

The Museum of Science and Industry in Manchester

The National Endowment for Science, Technology and the Arts

The National Galleries of Scotland

The National Gallery

The National Heritage Memorial Fund

The National Library of Scotland

The National Library of Wales

The National Lottery Charities Board

The National Maritime Museum

National Museums and Galleries on Merseyside

National Museums and Galleries of Wales

National Museums of Scotland

The National Portrait Gallery

The Natural History Museum

The Registrar of Public Lending Right

Resource: The Council for Museums, Archives and Libraries

The Royal Armouries

The Royal Botanic Garden, Edinburgh

The Royal Botanic Gardens, Kew

The Royal Commission on Ancient and Historical Monuments of Scotland

The Royal Commission on Ancient and Historical Monuments of Wales

The Royal Commission on Historical Manuscripts

The Royal Fine Art Commission for Scotland

The Science Museum

The Scottish Arts Council

Scottish Natural Heritage

Scottish Screen

Scottish Sports Council

The Scottish Tourist Board

Sir John Soane's Museum

Sport England

The Sports Council for Wales

The Tate Gallery

The Theatres Trust

The Treasure Valuation Committee

The UK Sports Council

The Victoria and Albert Museum

The Wales Tourist Board

The Wallace Collection

Public corporations and nationalised industries

The Bank of England, in respect of its public functions

The British Broadcasting Corporation, in respect of its public functions

The Broadcasting Standards Commission, in respect of its public functions

The Channel Four Television Corporation, in respect of its public functions

The Civil Aviation Authority

The Coal Authority

The Covent Garden Market Authority

A customer service committee maintained under section 28 of the Water Industry Act 1991

The Independent Television Commission, in respect of its public functions

The Radio Authority, in respect of its public functions

Sianel Pedwar Cymru (Welsh Fourth Channel Authority), in respect of its public functions

The United Kingdom Atomic Energy Authority, in respect of its public functions

Regulatory, audit and inspection

The Accounts Commission for Scotland

The Advisory, Conciliation and Arbitration Service (ACAS)

The Association of Authorised Public Accountants

The Association of Certified Chartered Accountants

The Association of Child Psychotherapy

The Audit Commission for Local Authorities and the National Health Service in England and Wales

Audit Scotland

The British Hallmarking Council

The British Standards Institute

The Chartered Institute of Patent Agents, in respect of its public functions

The Council for Licensed Conveyancers, in respect of its public functions

The Engineering Council

The Financial Services Authority

The General Chiropractic Council

The General Council of the Bar of England and Wales, in respect of its public functions

The General Dental Council

The General Medical Council

The General Optical Council

The General Osteopathic Council

The General Social Care Council

The Insolvency Practitioners Association

The Institute of Chartered Accountants in England and Wales

The Institute of Chartered Accountants of Scotland

The Institute of Legal Executives, in respect of its public functions

The Institute of Trade Mark Attorneys

The Law Society of England and Wales, in respect of its public functions

The Law Society of Scotland, in respect of its public functions

Her Majesty's Magistrates' Courts Service Inspectorate

The Master of the Court of the Faculties of the Archbishop of Canterbury, in respect of its public functions

The National Audit Office

The Royal Pharmaceutical Society of Great Britain, in respect of its statutory functions and the regulation of the pharmacy profession

The United Kingdom Central Council for Nursing, Midwifery and Health Visiting, in respect of its public functions

Research

The Alcohol Education and Research Council

The Apple and Pear Research Council

The Biotechnology and Biological Sciences Research Council

The Council for the Central Laboratory of the Research Councils

The Economic and Social Research Council

The Engineering and Physical Sciences Research Council

The Fire Service Research and Training Trust

The Horticultural Development Council

The Medical Research Council

The Natural Environment Research Council

The Particle Physics and Astronomy Research Council

Other bodies, etc

The Advisory Committee on Hazardous Substances

The Advisory Committee on Pesticides

The Advisory Committee on Releases to the Environment

The Advisory Council on the Misuse of Drugs

An agricultural dwelling house advisory committee established under the Rent (Agriculture) Act 1976

The Agricultural Wages Board for England and Wales

An Agricultural Wages Committee

The Animal Procedures Committee

A board of visitors established under section 6(2) of the Prison Act 1952

The Britain-Russia Centre

The British Association for Central and Eastern Europe

The British Council

The British Potato Council

The British Waterways Board

The British Wool Marketing Board

The Building Regulations Advisory Committee

The Building Standards Advisory Committee

The Central Advisory Committee on War Pensions

The Children and Family Court Advisory and Support Service

The Civil Justice Council

The Civil Procedure Rule Committee

The Commission for Racial Equality

The Commissioner for Local Administration in Scotland

The Commonwealth Scholarship Commission in the United Kingdom

The Community Development Foundation

The Consumer Council for Postal Services

The Council on Tribunals

The Criminal Injuries Compensation Authority

The Crofters' Commission

The Crown Court Rule Committee

The Deer Commission for Scotland

The Disability Living Allowance Advisory Board

The Disability Rights Commission

The Disabled Persons Transport Advisory Committee

The Electoral Commission

English Partnerships

The Environment Agency

The Environment Agency Advisory Committee for Wales

The Equal Opportunities Commission

The Family Proceedings Rule Committee

The Firearms Consultative Committee

The Fisheries (Electricity) Committee

Food From Britain

The Gaming Board for Great Britain

The Gas and Electricity Consumer Council

The Government Hospitality Advisory Committee for the Purchase of Wine

The Great Britain-China Centre

The Health and Safety Commission

The Health and Safety Executive

The Hill Farming Advisory Committee for Scotland

The Hill Farming Advisory Sub-Committee for Wales

The Home-Grown Cereals Authority

The Honours Scrutiny Committee

The Horserace Betting Levy Board

The Horserace Totalisator Board

The Industrial Injuries Advisory Council

The Information Commissioner

The Inland Waterways Amenity Advisory Council

The Insolvency Rules Committee

Investors in People UK

The Joint Nature Conservation Committee

The Land Registration Rule Committee

The Law Commission

The Legal Services Commission

The Legal Services Consultative Panel

The Local Government Boundary Commission for Scotland

The Local Government Boundary Commission for Wales

The Local Government Commission for England

The Low Pay Commission

The Magistrates' Courts Rule Committee

The Marshall Aid Commemoration Commission

The Meat and Livestock Commission

The Milk Development Council

The National Consumer Council

The National Forest Company

The National Radiological Protection Board

The New Opportunities Fund

The Northern Lighthouse Board

The Oil and Pipelines Agency

The Overseas Service Pensions Scheme Advisory Board

A regional flood defence committee established under section 14 of the Environment Act 1995

The Scottish Agricultural Wages Board

The Scottish Conveyancing and Executry Services Board

The Scottish Environment Protection Agency

The Scottish Industrial Development Advisory Board

The Scottish Law Commission

The Scottish Legal Aid Board

The Scottish Parliamentary Corporate Body

The Scottish Records Advisory Council

The Sea Fish Industry Authority

The Sentencing Advisory Panel

The Social Security Advisory Committee

The Strategic Rail Authority

The Trinity House Lighthouse Service

A visiting committee appointed under section 152 of the Immigration and Asylum Act 1999 for an immigration detention centre

The Wales New Deal Advisory Task Force

A War Pensions Committee

The Water Industry Commissioner for Scotland

The Welsh Development Agency

The Welsh Industrial Development Advisory Board

The Welsh Language Board

The Welsh Scientific Advisory Committee

The Westminster Foundation for Democracy

The Wilton Park Academic Council

The Wine Standards Board of the Vintners' Company

The Youth Justice Board for England and Wales

Appendix 2

Public authorities required to publish a race equality scheme

An assembly subsidiary as defined by section 99(4) of the Government of Wales Act 1998

The Audit Commission for Local Authorities and the National Health Service in England and Wales

A body corporate established pursuant to an order under section 67 of the Local Government Act 1985 (transfer of functions to successors of residuary bodies, etc)

The British Broadcasting Corporation, in respect of its public functions

The British Transport Police

The Broadcasting Standards Commission, in respect of its public functions

The Channel Four Television Corporation, in respect of its public functions

The Chief Constable for the Ministry of Defence Police appointed by the Secretary of State under section 1(3) of the Ministry of Defence Police Act 1987

A chief constable of a police force maintained under section 2 of the Police Act 1996

The Children and Family Court Advisory and Support Service

The Commissioner of Police for the City of London

The Commissioner of Police of the Metropolis

The Commission for Health Improvement

The Commission for Racial Equality

The Common Council of the City of London, in its capacity as a local authority or port health authority

The Common Council of the City of London, in its capacity as a police authority

The Council of the Isles of Scilly

In England, a county council, a London borough council or a district council

In Wales, a county council or a county borough council

The Disability Rights Commission

English Partnerships

The Equal Opportunities Commission

A fire authority constituted by a combination scheme under section 5 or 6 of the Fire Services Act 1947

The Greater London Authority

A health authority established under section 8 of the National Health Service Act 1977

The Health and Safety Commission

The Health and Safety Executive

The Higher Education Funding Council for Wales

The Higher Education Funding Council for England

A housing action trust established under Part III of the Housing Act 1988

The Housing Corporation

The Independent Television Commission, in respect of its public functions

A joint authority established under Part IV of the Local Government Act 1985 (fire services, civil defence and transport)

A joint authority established under section 21 of the Local Government Act 1992

The Learning and Skills Council for England

The Legal Services Commission

The Local Government Commission for England

A local probation board established under section 4 of the Criminal Justice and Court Services Act 2000

The London Development Agency

The London Fire and Emergency Planning Authority

A magistrates' courts committee established under section 27 of the Justices of the Peace Act 1997

The Metropolitan Police Authority established under section 5B of the Police Act 1996

A Minister of the Crown or government department

The National Assembly for Wales

The National Audit Office

The National Council for Education and Training for Wales

A National Health Service trust established under section 5 of the National Health Service and Community Care Act 1990

Any of the naval, military or air forces of the Crown

A passenger transport executive for a passenger transport area (within the meaning of Part II of the Transport Act 1968)

A police authority established under section 3 of the Police Act 1996

The Police Complaints Authority

A primary care trust established under section 16A of the National Health Service Act 1977

The Radio Authority, in respect of its public functions

A regional development agency established under the Regional Development Agencies Act 1998 (other than the London Development Agency)

The Scottish Parliamentary Corporate Body

The Service Authority for the National Crime Squad

The Service Authority for the National Criminal Intelligence Service, otherwise than in respect of its Scottish functions (within the meaning given by section L2 of Part II of Schedule 5 to the Scotland Act 1998)

Sianel Pedwar Cymru (Welsh Fourth Channel Authority), in respect of its public functions

A special health authority established under section 11 of the National Health Service Act 1977

The Strategic Rail Authority

The Sub-Treasurer of the Inner Temple or the Under-Treasurer of the Middle Temple, in his capacity as a local authority

Transport for London

The Welsh Development Agency

Appendix 3:
Public authorities bound by the employment duty

Ministers of the Crown and government departments

(1) A Minister of the Crown or government department
(2) Sub-paragraph (1) does not include the Security Service, the Intelligence Service or the Government Communications Headquarters

Scottish Administration

(1) An office-holder in the Scottish Administration (within the meaning given by section 126(7)(a) of the Scotland Act 1998)
(2) Members of the staff of the Scottish Administration (within the meaning given by section 126(7)(b) of that Act)

National Assembly for Wales

(1) The National Assembly for Wales
(2) An Assembly subsidiary as defined by section 99(4) of the Government of Wales Act 1998

Armed Forces

Any of the naval, military or air forces of the Crown

National Health Service: England and Wales

A health authority established under section 8 of the National Health Service Act 1977

A National Health Service trust established under section 5 of the National Health Service and Community Care Act 1990

A primary care trust established under section 16A of that Act

A special health authority established under section 11 of that Act

Local government

A body corporate established pursuant to an order under section 67 of the Local Government Act 1985 (transfer of functions to successors of residuary bodies, etc)

A body corporate established pursuant to an order under section 22 of the Local Government Act 1992 (residuary bodies)

The Broads Authority established by section 1 of the Norfolk and Suffolk Broads Act 1988

Any charter trustees constituted under section 246 of that Act

The Common Council of the City of London in its capacity as a local authority or port health authority

The Council of the Isles of Scilly

A fire authority constituted by a combination scheme under section 5 or 6 of the Fire Services Act 1947

The Greater London Authority

An internal drainage board which is continued in being by virtue of section 1 of the Land Drainage Act 1991

A joint authority established under Part IV of the Local Government Act 1985 (fire services, civil defence and transport)

A joint authority established under section 21 of the Local Government Act 1992

A joint board which is continued in being by virtue of section 263(1) of that Act

A joint committee constituted in accordance with section 102(1)(b) of the Local Government Act 1972

A joint planning board constituted for an area in Wales outside a National Park by an order under section 2(1B) of the Town and Country Planning Act 1990

A local authority (within the meaning of the Local Government Act 1972), namely
(a) in England, a county council, a London borough council, a district council;
(b) in Wales, a county council, a county borough council

A local probation board established under section 4 of the Criminal Justice and Court Services Act 2000

The London Development Agency

The London Fire and Emergency Planning Authority

A magistrates' courts committee established under section 27 of the Justices of the Peace Act 1997

A national park authority established by an order under section 63 of the Environment Act 1995

A passenger transport executive for a passenger transport area (within the meaning of Part II of the Transport Act 1968)

A port health authority constituted by an order under section 2 of the Public Health (Control of Disease) Act 1984

A regional development agency established under the Regional Development Agencies Act 1998 (other than the London Development Agency)

The Sub-Treasurer of the Inner Temple or the Under-Treasurer of the Middle Temple, in his capacity as a local authority

Transport for London

A waste disposal authority established by virtue of an order under section 10(1) of the Local Government Act 1985

Education

The Adult Learning Inspectorate

The British Educational Communication and Technology Agency

The Construction Industry Training Board

The Engineering Construction Industry Training Board

The General Teaching Council for Scotland

The General Teaching Council for Wales

The Higher Education Funding Council for England

The Higher Education Funding Council for Wales

The Learning and Skills Council for England

The managers of a grant-aided school (within the meaning of section 135 of the Education (Scotland) Act 1980)

The National Council for Education and Training for Wales

The Qualifications and Curriculum Authority

The Qualifications, Curriculum and Assessment Authority for Wales

The Student Loans Company

The Teacher Training Agency

Housing bodies

A housing action trust established under Part III of the Housing Act 1988

The Housing Corporation

Police

The British Transport Police

A chief constable of a police force maintained under section 2 of the Police Act 1996

The Chief Constable for the Ministry of Defence Police appointed by the Secretary of State under section 1(3) of the Ministry of Defence Police Act 1987

The Commissioner of Police for the City of London

The Commissioner of Police of the Metropolis

The Common Council of the City of London in its capacity as a police authority

The Metropolitan Police Authority established under section 5B of the Police Act 1996

A police authority established under section 3 of the Police Act 1996

The Police Complaints Authority

The Police Information Technology Organisation

A selection panel for independent members of police authorities

The Service Authority for the National Crime Squad

The Service Authority for the National Criminal Intelligence Service

Health

The Commission for Health Improvement

The Council for Professions Supplementary to Medicine, in respect of its public functions

The Dental Practice Board

The English National Board for Nursing, Midwifery and Health Visiting

The Human Fertilisation and Embryology Authority

The Joint Committee on Postgraduate Training for General Practice

The National Biological Standards Board

The Public Health Laboratory Service Board

The Royal College of Anaesthetists, in respect of its public functions

The Royal College of General Practitioners, in respect of its public functions

The Royal College of Midwives, in respect of its public functions

The Royal College of Nursing, in respect of its public functions

The Royal College of Obstetricians and Gynaecologists, in respect of its public functions

The Royal College of Ophthalmologists, in respect of its public functions

The Royal College of Paediatrics and Child Health, in respect of its public functions

The Royal College of Pathologists, in respect of its public functions

The Royal College of Physicians, in respect of its public functions

The Royal College of Psychiatrists, in respect of its public functions

The Royal College of Radiologists, in respect of its public functions

The Royal College of Speech and Language Therapists, in respect of its public functions

The Royal College of Surgeons of England, in respect of its public functions

The Specialist Training Authority of the Medical Royal Colleges

The Welsh National Board for Nursing, Midwifery and Health Visiting

Libraries, museums and arts

The Arts Council of England

The Arts Council of Wales

The British Library

The British Museum

The British Tourist Authority

The Commission for Architecture and the Built Environment

The Countryside Council for Wales

The Design Council

English Nature

The English Tourist Board

The Film Council

The Geffrye Museum

The Historic Buildings and Monuments Commission for England

The Historic Royal Palaces Trust

The Horniman Museum

The Imperial War Museum

The Library and Information Services Council (Wales)

The Millennium Commission

The Museum of London

The Museum of Science and Industry in Manchester

The National Endowment for Science, Technology and the Arts

The National Gallery

The National Heritage Memorial Fund

The National Library of Wales

The National Lottery Charities Board

The National Maritime Museum

National Museums and Galleries on Merseyside

National Museums and Galleries of Wales

The National Portrait Gallery

The Natural History Museum

The Registrar of Public Lending Right

Resource: The Council for Museums, Archives and Libraries

The Royal Armouries

The Royal Botanic Gardens, Kew

The Royal Commission on Ancient and Historical Monuments of Wales

The Royal Commission on Historical Manuscripts

The Science Museum

Sir John Soane's Museum

Sport England

The Sports Council for Wales

The Tate Gallery

The UK Sports Council

The Victoria and Albert Museum

The Wales Tourist Board

The Wallace Collection

Public corporations and nationalised industries

The Bank of England, in respect of its public functions

The British Broadcasting Corporation, in respect of its public functions

The Broadcasting Standards Commission, in respect of its public functions

The Channel Four Television Corporation, in respect of its public functions

The Civil Aviation Authority

The Coal Authority

The Covent Garden Market Authority

A Customer Service Committee maintained under section 28 of the Water Industry Act 1991

The Independent Television Commission, in respect of its public functions

The Radio Authority, in respect of its public functions

Sianel Pedwar Cymru (Welsh Fourth Channel Authority), in respect of its public functions

The United Kingdom Atomic Energy Authority, in respect of its public functions

Regulatory, audit and inspection

The Advisory, Conciliation and Arbitration Service (ACAS)

The Association of Authorised Public Accountants

The Association of Certified Chartered Accountants

The Association of Child Psychotherapy

The Audit Commission for Local Authorities and the National Health Service in England and Wales

The British Hallmarking Council

The British Standards Institute

The Chartered Institute of Patent Agents, in respect of its public functions

The Council for Licensed Conveyancers, in respect of its public functions

The Engineering Council

The Financial Services Authority

The General Chiropractic Council

The General Council of the Bar of England and Wales, in respect of its public functions

The General Dental Council

The General Medical Council

The General Optical Council

The General Osteopathic Council

The General Social Care Council

The Insolvency Practitioners Association

The Institute of Chartered Accountants in England and Wales

The Institute of Legal Executives, in respect of its public functions

The Institute of Trade Mark Attorneys

The Law Society of England and Wales, in respect of its public functions

Her Majesty's Magistrates' Courts Service Inspectorate

The Master of the Court of the Faculties of the Archbishop of Canterbury, in respect of its public functions

The National Audit Office

The Royal Pharmaceutical Society of Great Britain, in respect of its statutory functions and the regulation of the pharmacy profession

The United Kingdom Central Council for Nursing, Midwifery and Health Visiting, in respect of its public functions

Research

The Alcohol Education and Research Council

The Apple and Pear Research Council

The Biotechnology and Biological Sciences Research Council

The Council for the Central Laboratory of the Research Councils

The Economic and Social Research Council

The Engineering and Physical Sciences Research Council

The Fire Service Research and Training Trust

The Horticultural Development Council

The Medical Research Council

The Natural Environment Research Council

The Particle Physics and Astronomy Research Council

Other bodies, etc

A board of visitors established under section 6(2) of the Prison Act 1952

The Britain-Russia Centre

The British Association for Central and Eastern Europe

The British Council

The British Potato Council

The British Waterways Board

The British Wool Marketing Board

The Children and Family Court Advisory and Support Service

The Commission for Racial Equality

The Community Development Foundation

The Criminal Injuries Compensation Authority

The Disability Rights Commission

The Electoral Commission

English Partnerships

The Environment Agency

The Equal Opportunities Commission

Food From Britain

The Gaming Board for Great Britain

The Gas and Electricity Consumer Council

The Great Britain-China Centre

The Health and Safety Commission

The Health and Safety Executive

The Home-Grown Cereals Authority

The Horserace Betting Levy Board

The Horserace Totalisator Board

The Information Commissioner

Investors in People UK

The Joint Nature Conservation Committee

The Legal Services Commission

The Local Government Commission for England

The Marshall Aid Commemoration Commission

The Meat and Livestock Commission

The Milk Development Council

The National Consumer Council

The National Forest Company

The National Radiological Protection Board

The New Opportunities Fund

The Northern Lighthouse Board

The Oil and Pipelines Agency

The Sea Fish Industry Authority

The Strategic Rail Authority

The Trinity House Lighthouse Service

A visiting committee appointed under section 152 of the Immigration and Asylum Act 1999 for an immigration detention centre

The Welsh Development Agency

The Welsh Language Board

The Westminster Foundation for Democracy

The Wine Standards Board of the Vintners' Company

The Youth Justice Board for England and Wales

Appendix 4

Public authorities bound by the duties for educational institutions

Part I

The governing body of an educational establishment maintained by a local education authority

The governing body of a city technology college, city college for technology of the arts, or a city academy

Part II

The governing body of an institution within the further education sector (within the meaning of section 91(3) of the Further and Higher Education Act 1992)

The governing body of an institution within the higher education sector (within the meaning of section 91(5) of the Further and Higher Education Act 1992)

Part III

A local education authority

Part IV

The Department for Education and Skills

Part V

The Learning and Skills Council for England

The Higher Education Funding Council for England

The Higher Education Funding Council for Wales

The National Council for Education and Training for Wales

Appendix 5
Scottish public authorities

The Accounts Commission for Scotland

The Advisory Committee on Sites of Special Scientific Interest

The Ancient Monuments Board for Scotland

Audit Scotland

The board of management of a self-governing school (within the meaning of the Self-Governing Schools etc (Scotland) Act 1989)

The Building Standards Advisory Committee

A chief officer of police appointed under section 4 of the Police (Scotland) Act 1967

A college of further education maintained by an education authority in the exercise of its further education functions in providing courses of further education (within the meaning of section 1(5)(b)(ii) of the Education (Scotland) Act 1980)

A college of further education with a board of management (within the meaning of section 36(1) of the Further and Higher Education (Scotland) Act 1992)

The Commissioner for Local Administration in Scotland

The Common Services Agency for the NHS in Scotland

A community council established under section 51 of the Local Government (Scotland) Act 1973

A council constituted under section 2 of the Local Government etc (Scotland) Act 1994

The Crofters Commission

The Fisheries (Electricity) Committee

The General Teaching Council for Scotland

The governing body of an institution within the higher education sector (within the meaning of Part II of the Further and Higher Education (Scotland) Act 1992)

A health board constituted under section 2 of the National Health Service (Scotland) Act 1978

The Hill Farming Advisory Committee for Scotland

The Historic Buildings Council for Scotland

The Institute of Chartered Accountants of Scotland

A joint board (within the meaning of section 235(1) of the Local Government (Scotland) Act 1973)

The Law Society of Scotland, in respect of its public functions

Learning and Teaching Scotland

A licensing board constituted under section 1 of the Licensing (Scotland) Act 1976

The Local Government Boundary Commission for Scotland

The managers of a central institution (within the meaning of section 135 of the Education (Scotland) Act 1980)

The managers of a grant-aided school (within the meaning of section 135 of the Education (Scotland) Act 1980)

A member of the staff of the Scottish Administration (within the meaning given by section 126(7)(b) of the Scotland Act 1998)

The Mental Welfare Commission for Scotland

National Galleries of Scotland

A National Health Service trust established under section 12A of the National Health Service (Scotland) Act 1978

The National Library of Scotland

National Museums of Scotland

Newbattle Abbey College

A police authority established under section 2 of the Police (Scotland) Act 1967

The Royal Botanic Garden, Edinburgh

The Royal Commission on the Ancient and Historical Monuments of Scotland

The Royal Fine Art Commission for Scotland

Sabhal Mòr Ostaig College

An office-holder in the Scottish Administration (within the meaning given by section 126(7)(a) of the Scotland Act 1998)

The Scottish Agricultural Wages Board

The Scottish Arts Council

The Scottish Conveyancing and Executry Services Board

The Scottish Dental Practice Board

Scottish Enterprise, and Highlands and Islands Enterprise, established under the Enterprise and New Towns (Scotland) Act 1990

The Scottish Environment Protection Agency

The Scottish Further Education Funding Council

The Scottish Further Education Unit, in respect of its public functions

The Scottish Higher Education Funding Council

The Scottish Hospital Endowments Research Trust

The Scottish Hospital Trust

The Scottish Industrial Development Advisory Board

The Scottish Law Commission

The Scottish Legal Aid Board

The Scottish Medical Practices Committee

Scottish Natural Heritage

The Scottish Qualifications Authority

The Scottish Records Advisory Council

Scottish Screen

The Scottish Tourist Board

A special health board constituted under section 2 of the National Health Service (Scotland) Act 1978

Sportscotland (Scottish Sports Council)

A water or sewerage authority constituted under section 62 of the Local Government etc (Scotland) Act 1994

The Deer Commission for Scotland

The Water Industry Commissioner for Scotland

Appendix 6
Other guidance published by the CRE

Guides on the duty to promote race equality

The Duty to Promote Race Equality: A guide for public authorities (2002)
>A non-statutory guide to the Code of Practice on the Duty to Promote Race Equality.

The Duty to Promote Race Equality: A guide for schools (2002)
>A non-statutory guide to the Code of Practice on the Duty to Promote Race Equality.

The Duty to Promote Race Equality: A guide for further and higher education institutions (2002)
>A non-statutory guide to the Code of Practice on the Duty to Promote Race Equality.

Ethnic Monitoring: A guide for public authorities (2002)
>A non-statutory guide to the Code of Practice on the Duty to Promote Race Equality.

Other statutory CRE codes

Code of Practice for the Elimination of Racial Discrimination and the Promotion of Equality of Opportunity in Employment (1984)
>This code stays in force. The Race Relations Act 1976 (Statutory Duties) Order 2001 gives public authorities new responsibilities for monitoring employment practice.

Code of Practice in Rented Housing: For the elimination of racial discrimination and the promotion of equal opportunities (1991)
>This code stays in force.

Code of Practice in Non-Rented (Owner-Occupied) Housing: For the elimination of racial discrimination and the promotion of equal opportunities (1992)
>This code stays in force. The Race Relations Act 1976 (Statutory Duties) Order 2001 gives public authorities new responsibilities for promoting race equality.

Non-statutory CRE codes

Code of Practice for the Elimination of Racial Discrimination in Education (England and Wales) (1989)
>This code should be read together with the statutory Code of Practice on the Duty to Promote Race Equality.

Code of Practice for the Elimination of Racial Discrimination in Education (Scotland) (1989)
>This code should be read together with the statutory Code of Practice on the Duty to Promote Race Equality.

Code of Practice in Maternity Services: For the elimination of racial discrimination and the promotion of equal opportunities (1994)
>This code should be read together with the statutory Code of Practice on the Duty to Promote Race Equality.

Code of Practice in Primary Health Care: For the elimination of racial discrimination and the promotion of equal opportunities (1992)
>This code should be read together with the statutory Code of Practice on the Duty to Promote Race Equality.

Standards for racial equality

Learning for All: Standards for racial equality in schools in England and Wales (2000)
Schools should continue to use these standards, which support the statutory Code of Practice on the Duty to Promote Race Equality.

Equality Standard for Local Government in England and Wales (2001)
This standard, which supports the statutory Code of Practice on the Duty to Promote Race Equality, has replaced *Racial Equality Means Quality: A standard for racial equality for local government in England and Wales.*

Racial Equality Means Quality: A standard for racial equality for local government in Scotland (1995)
Local government should continue to use this standard, which supports the statutory Code of Practice on the Duty to Promote Race Equality.